NATIONAL ANIMALS

by Rosie Colosi

SCHOLASTIC INC.

ISBN 978-1-338-65218-5

10 9 8 7 6 5 4 3 2 1   20 21 22 23 24

Printed in the U.S.A.   40

First printing, October 2020

Designed by Jennifer Rinaldi

Photos ©: cover center left: W. Perry Conway/Getty Images; cover bottom right: AGAMI Photo Agency/Alamy Stock Photo; 1 top left: blickwinkel/Alamy Stock Photo; 10 top left: 1001slide/Getty Images; 11 center: Henning Kaiser/picture alliance/Getty Images; 11 bottom: cgwp.co.uk/Alamy Stock Photo; 12 center: blickwinkel/Alamy Stock Photo; 12 bottom: Top-Pics TBK/Alamy Stock Photo; 13 center: Picture by Tambako the Jaguar/Getty Images; 17 center: Friedrich von Hörsten/Alamy Stock Photo; 17 bottom: Johannes Gerhardus Swanepoel/Dreamstime; 18 center: WLDavies/Getty Images; 18 bottom: WLDavies/Getty Images; 26 center: JackF/Fotosearch LBRF/age fotostock; 26 bottom: Alexey Bubryak/Photolibrary/Getty Images; 27 center: Nimit Virdi/Getty Images; 28 bottom: Marek Mihulka Photography/Dreamstime; 30 center: Freder/Getty Images; 30 bottom: imageBROKER/Alamy Stock Photo; 31 center: blickwinkel/Alamy Stock Photo; 32 center: Urban Napflin/Alamy Stock Photo; 33 center: cinoby/Getty Images; 33 bottom: Vkilikov/Dreamstime; 34 bottom: WILDLIFE GmbH/Alamy Stock Photo; 35 center: tony mills/Alamy Stock Photo; 37 center: Ben Queenborough/Getty Images; 37 bottom: WILDLIFE GmbH/Alamy Stock Photo; 38 bottom: David Chapman/Alamy Stock Photo; 41 center: Zoltan Szilvas/500px/Getty Images; 41 bottom: Danita Delimont/Alamy Stock Photo; 42 center: W. Perry Conway/Getty Images; 43 center: Yggdrasill33/Dreamstime; 43 bottom: Bernard Golden/Alamy Stock Photo; 45 center: Ignacio Palacios/Getty Images; 45 bottom: guenterguni/Getty Images; 47 bottom: Saliken/Getty Images; 48 center: Jana Telenská/Dreamstime; 48 bottom: Sergey Uryadnikov/Dreamstime; 49 center: silvia cozzi/Alamy Stock Photo; 49 bottom: blickwinkel/Alamy Stock Photo; 51 center: James R.D. Scott/Getty Images; 51 bottom: Carol Grant/Getty Images; 52 center: blickwinkel/Alamy Stock Photo; 52 bottom: AGAMI Photo Agency/Alamy Stock Photo; 53 center: AGAMI Photo Agency/Alamy Stock Photo; 53 bottom: Rolf Nussbaumer Photography/Alamy Stock Photo; 54 bottom: Auscape/Getty Images; 56 center: Wolfgang Kaehler/Getty Images; 58 center left: Guy Bartov/Alamy Stock Photo; 59 center: O. Alamany & E. Vicens/Getty Images; 59 bottom: Nature Picture Library/Alamy Stock Photo; 60 center: Christa Fredriksson/Lonely Planet/Getty Images; 61 bottom: Mark Jones Roving Tortoise Photos/Getty Images; 62 center: Ben Schonewille/Dreamstime; 62 bottom: Ivan Kuzmin/Getty Images. All other photos © Shutterstock.com.

NATIONAL ANIMALS

(Furry, Feathered, Flying!)

NORTH
AMERICA

ATLANTIC
OCEAN

SOUTH
AMERICA

PACIFIC OCEAN

SOUTHERN OCEAN

(FURRY, FEATHERED, FLYING) WORLD!

ARCTIC OCEAN

ASIA

PACIFIC OCEAN

AFRICA

INDIAN OCEAN

AUSTRALIA/ OCEANIA

ANTARCTICA

ANIMALS AROUND THE WORLD

Some are adorable. Some are ferocious. Some are big. Some are small. And some are even mythical!

They're national animals!

A national animal is a symbol for a country, like the mascot of a sports team. When you see the Phanatic, it probably reminds you of the Philadelphia Phillies. When you see Big Red, you probably think of the Arizona Cardinals. Likewise, when you see a bald eagle, you might think of the United States of America.

The bald eagle is America's national *bird*. You see it on U.S. money and on America's Great Seal. The bald eagle signals that Americans value strength and freedom. The type of creature a country picks to be a national animal can tell you a little bit about its values and traits.

But did you know that the United States also has a national *mammal*? Over a third of countries that have a national animal have *more than just one* . . . they may have a national aquatic animal or even a national insect. And some countries have national animals that aren't *real*! Their national animals are based on myths, or traditional stories, from their country.

This book will be your guide to national animals around the world. You'll learn about 51 different animals and the countries that selected them. You can read the book from start to finish, tackle one continent at a time, or hop around from one country to another.

YOU'LL FIND OUT:

- which animal is known as **"the African unicorn"**
- which animal has a **black tongue**
- which animal has a nose **that keeps it warm**
- which animal can be **traced back in history for millions of years**
- which animal can **warn you when an earthquake is about to happen**
- which animal can ride **first-class on planes**

Travel the globe and learn more about these furry, fuzzy, feathered, flying animals!

15 MYTHICAL NATIONAL ANIMALS:

- **Austria:** Austrian Bundesadler "Federal Eagle"
- **Belgium:** Leo Belgicus "Belgic lion"
- **Bhutan:** Druk
- **China:** Druk
- **China:** Chinese dragon
- **Czech Republic:** Double-tailed lion
- **Germany:** Bundesadler "Federal Eagle"
- **Greece:** Phoenix
- **Hungary:** Turul
- **Indonesia:** Garuda
- **North Korea:** Chollima
- **Portugal:** Barcelos rooster
- **Russia:** Double-headed eagle
- **Scotland:** Unicorn
- **Serbia:** White eagle
- **Wales:** Y Ddraig Goch (Welsh dragon)

THE MOST POPULAR NATIONAL ANIMALS:

- **The Lion:** 15 countries chose to be represented by a lion because it represents strength.
- **The Eagle:** 8 countries chose an eagle. It represents confidence.
- **The Leopard and The Tiger:** These big cats were chosen by 4 countries each. They represent power and wisdom.

NOTE ABOUT OFFICIAL LANGUAGE:
Throughout this book, you'll learn the official languages of the countries presented. "Official Language" refers to a language given a special legal status in a country. It is the elected language used in government. For countries that don't have an official language, the national language, or the shared language used by the majority of the people in a particular area, is noted.

ALGERIA

Capital: Algiers
Official Languages: Amazigh, Arabic
Population: 42,654,000

FANCY FOOTWORK

The fennec fox's hairy feet act as "snowshoes" to stay on top of hot sand. They also act like shovels to help them dig down into their underground dens.

NATIONAL ANIMAL
FENNEC FOX

Height: 9.5–16 inches
Weight: 2.2–3.3 pounds
Top Speed: 20 miles per hour
Diet: plants, rodents, eggs, reptiles, and insects
Habitat: desert

The Sahara Desert covers much of Algeria, and this little fox has adapted to its harsh living conditions. The fox's big ears help keep it cool by giving off body heat. The fox is nocturnal, so it mostly sleeps while the sun is the hottest. It can survive for a long time without water— it gets the water it needs from fruits and leaves.

This fox lives in groups of about ten or so in **burrows**, or tunnels dug underneath the ground. They are very social and often talk to each other with whimpers, growls, and yells.

BOTSWANA

Capital: Gaborone
Official Language: English, Tswana
Population: 2,289,000

NATIONAL ANIMAL
ZEBRA

Height: about 4.5 feet
Weight: 550–700 pounds
Top Speed: 40 miles per hour
Diet: grasses, leaves, and young trees
Habitat: grasslands and savannas

FAR FROM HOME

Every year, zebras migrate from Tanzania to Kenya to find food and water—that's a distance of 1,800 miles!

The zebra, with its black-and-white stripes, represents the different backgrounds of people who live in Botswana—and their unity and cooperation with one another. Botswana's national soccer team is nicknamed "The Zebras," and the Botswana coat of arms features two zebras, showing the national pride for the animal. The zebra's stripes even inspired the design of the country's flag!

Those black-and-white stripes protect zebras from the hot African sun. The black stripes absorb sunlight, while the white stripes reflect it. Air moves at different speeds over each stripe, which creates air currents that keep the zebra cool. Those stripes also help distract predators.

CENTRAL AFRICAN REPUBLIC

Capital: Bangui
Official Languages: French, Sango
Population: 4,737,000

HEAR, HEAR!

An elephant can hear another elephant's call from up to 2.5 miles away!

NATIONAL ANIMAL
ELEPHANT

Height: up to 10 feet
Weight: up to 6.6 tons
Top Speed: 25 miles per hour
Diet: roots, grasses, fruit, and bark
Habitat: savannas, grasslands, forests, deserts, swamps, and tropical areas

African elephants are the largest land animals on Earth! You can tell them apart from Asian elephants because the shape of their ears looks like the continent of Africa. Those big ears help radiate heat and communicate with other elephants by flapping or moving in certain ways.

The African elephant has been hunted for its ivory tusks, which are made into things like jewelry and piano keys. There has been a large effort by the country to protect the elephants from poachers.

Because elephants are so big and strong, they are a perfect symbol of power. An elephant also appears on the Central African Republic's coat of arms.

DEMOCRATIC REPUBLIC OF THE CONGO

Capital: Kinshasa
Official Language: French
Population: 91,829,000

NATIONAL ANIMAL
OKAPI

Height: about 5 feet
Weight: 440–770 pounds
Top Speed: 37 miles per hour
Diet: leaves, twigs, and fruits
Habitat: rain forest

YUCK!

The okapi has stinky feet. Their feet leave a sticky, smelly, tar-like substance on the ground to mark their **territory**.

The okapi has become the symbol of **conservation** for the Congo's Ituri Forest due to it being **native** to the region. You can find its image throughout the country, on Congolese money and even on some water bottles!

The okapi may look like a zebra, but it actually belongs in the giraffe family. Like giraffes, the okapi has a long tongue—it's long enough to reach its ears and its eyes!

Okapis are sometimes called the "African unicorn" because it is so rare to find one. Even though the okapi's stripes look bold in the sunlight, they help the animal hide in the dense rain forest.

EGYPT

Capital: Cairo
Official Language: Arabic
Population: 98,976,000

This eagle steals food from other birds mid-flight.

NATIONAL BIRD

STEPPE EAGLE

Height: 2.2–2.6 feet
Weight: 3.3–8.6 pounds
Top Speed: 186 miles per hour on a dive
Diet: gophers, small birds, reptiles, and insects
Habitat: desert, savanna, and grassland steppes

You can find this strong bird on Egypt's flag. This eagle has beautiful features—a reddish-brown patch on its neck, and oval nostrils—that make it stand out from other eagles. It is generally quiet, but it sometimes makes a noise like a crow barking.

The steppe eagle prefers to eat fresh meat rather than rotted, dead carcasses. It is a very smart hunter—it can watch a mole rat burrow underground and then return to that spot and try to dig the animal out with its claws.

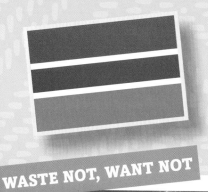

GAMBIA

Capital: Banjul
Official Language: English
Population: 2,184,000

NATIONAL ANIMAL

SPOTTED HYENA

Height: 2.5–2.6 feet
Weight: 88–190 pounds
Top Speed: 37 miles per hour
Diet: wildebeests, antelope, birds, lizards, snakes, and insects
Habitat: desert, savanna, swamp, and forest

WASTE NOT, WANT NOT

A hyena's dinner could be as much as one-third its body weight. They eat almost every part of their **prey**, including skin, hooves, bone, and teeth.

Gambia may be the smallest country in Africa, but it chose Africa's most successful predator, the spotted hyena, as its national animal. Gambia's national animal used to be the elephant, but it was hunted to extinction in the country almost 100 years ago.

Hyenas are skilled hunters with strong jaws who often compete with lions for food. They are smart, social, and efficient. They often live in groups of up to 80 hyenas.

Although hyenas look like dogs, they are more closely related to cats. They like to yell and cackle—sometimes they can be heard from a few miles away!

KENYA

Capital: Nairobi
Official Languages: English, Swahili
Population: 48,924,000

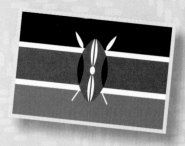

You can hear a lion's roar for up to five miles.

NATIONAL ANIMAL

LION

Height: 4.5–6.5 feet
Weight: 265–420 pounds
Top Speed: 50 miles per hour
Diet: large animals, like zebras and wildebeests
Habitat: plains, thick brush, and dry thorn forest

Kenya values the lion's strength and bravery. The lion appears on Kenya's coat of arms as a symbol of protection. Many tourists travel to Kenya to see lions at the Maasai Mara National Reserve.

Lions live in a pride that can include anywhere from 3 to 40 lions! Female lions usually do the hunting. Because lions often chase animals that are faster than they are, they work together to kill their food. While the females hunt, the males defend their territory.

MADAGASCAR

Capital: Antananarivo
Official Languages: French, Malagasy
Population: 24,981,000

NATIONAL ANIMAL

RING-TAILED LEMUR

EAU DE LEMUR

Height: 17.75 inches
Weight: 5-7.5 pounds
Top Speed: 12 miles per hour
Diet: leaves, flowers, insects, fruit, herbs, and small animals
Habitat: arid, open areas, and forests

Lemurs use their unique scent to communicate, mark their territory, and compete with one another.

These **primates** are only found on the island of Madagascar. Their exclusivity to the island is why Madagascar chose them as the national animal.

Lemurs are very social animals and make all sorts of funny faces to communicate with one another. They also enjoy sunbathing—they sit upright with their underside facing the sun. Most lemurs spend a lot of time in trees, but ring-tailed lemurs spend almost half of their time on the ground. When they travel, they keep their tails raised in the air to keep their group together.

RWANDA

Capital: Kigali
Official Languages: English, French, Kinyarwanda, Swahili
Population: 12,090,000

BATHING BEAUTIES

Leopards are one of the few cats that like water—and they're strong swimmers, too!

AFRICAN LEOPARD

Height: 2–2.5 feet
Weight: 37–143 pounds
Top Speed: 35–37 miles per hou
Diet: meat, fish, reptiles, birds, rodents, hares, warthogs, antelopes, and baboons
Habitat: desert and semidesert regions, savanna grasslands, mountains, rain forests, and occasionally cities

With its grace, balance, and strength, the solitary leopard is a powerful reflection of Rwanda's people.

Leopards are great tree-climbers. To keep lions and hyenas from stealing their food, they'll often store it high up in tree branches. A leopard can climb as high as 50 feet while carrying an animal bigger than itself!

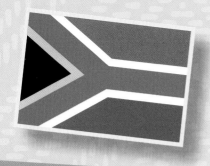

SOUTH AFRICA

Capitals: Pretoria (administrative), Cape Town (legislative), Bloemfontein (judicial)
Official Languages: Afrikaans, English, Ndebele, Sepedi, Sotho, Swazi, Tsonga, Tswana, Venda, Xhosa, Zulu
Population: 57,142,000

NATIONAL ANIMAL
SPRINGBOK

Shoulder Height: 27–34 inches
Weight: 59–106 pounds
Top Speed: 55 miles per hour
Diet: leaves, flowering plants, and melons
Habitat: open grassland

HIDDEN HAIR

The springbok has a hidden patch of white hair on its back that you can only see when the animal pronks.

The springbok is a type of gazelle that represents speed and perseverance. You can see the springbok's image on South African airplanes, Ranger cars, and the coat of arms. It even became the name for the national rugby team: "the Springboks."

The springbok gets its name from the Afrikaans words *spring* ("jump") and *bok* ("goat"). The animal has a special type of jumping display. It jumps with an arched back and stiff legs. This is called "pronking."

TANZANIA

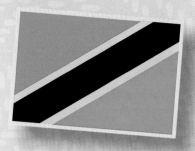

Capitals: Dar es Salaam (administrative), Dodoma (legislative)
Official Languages: English, Swahili
Population: 55,451,343

Giraffes have black tongues to protect them from getting sunburned while they eat.

NATIONAL ANIMAL
MASAI GIRAFFE

Height: 16–19 feet
Weight: 2,600–4,250 pounds
Top Speed: 35 miles per hour
Diet: acacia leaves
Habitat: savanna

The giraffe represents strength, flexibility, and clear vision. Sometimes called "Africa's gentle giant," the giraffe symbolizes seeing the world in a new way. Because giraffes are decreasing in numbers, June 21 has been named World Giraffe Day—it reminds us to save the tallest animal on the longest day of the year.

The pattern of a giraffe's coat is as unique as a human's fingerprints. Scientists think that giraffe mothers pass on the smoothness and roundness of their spots to their children.

BRING IT ON

Capital: Harare
Official Languages: Chewa,
Chibarwe, English, Kalanga,
Koisan, Nambya, Ndau, Ndebele,
Shangani, Shona, sign language,
Sotho, Tsonga, Tswana,
Venda, Xhosa
Population: 14,370,000

NATIONAL ANIMAL
SABLE ANTELOPE

Height: 45–56 inches
Weight: 485–525 pounds
Top Speed: 35 miles per hour
Diet: grass, herbs, and leaves
from shrubs and trees
Habitat: "miombo," a mixture
of bush and grassland

The sable antelope's horns can grow to be over five feet long! They develop a new ring on their horns every year.

This stunning antelope has horns that make it a prize snap for photographers. Zimbabwe takes pride in its unique and beautiful appearance and protects it in nature parks where hunting is banned. The word *sable* means "black" or "dark color," and it refers to the antelope's dark coat.

This animal moves in herds of 20–30 females, their young, and one male, who will challenge any other male he sees. Its main predator is the leopard.

ANTARCTICA

Capital: Antarctica does not have a capital city—or any cities at all!
Official Languages: Various based on the changing population - some include English, German, Maori, Norwegian, Russian, and Swedish
Population: 1,000–5,000, depending on the time of year

NATIONAL ANIMAL
PENGUIN

Height: 1.3–3.7 feet
Weight: 2.2–90 pounds
Top Speed: 22 miles per hour
Diet: squid, fish, and krill (small shrimplike animals)
Habitat: islands and remote regions in the Southern Hemisphere

AH-CHOO!

Penguins can drink seawater when they're thirsty. A special gland above their eye gets rid of some of the salt, and any leftover salt gets sprayed out when they sneeze!

Penguins only live in the Southern Hemisphere in places where there aren't many land predators, so they tend to be friendly animals that aren't afraid of humans. They form lifelong relationships with one another, and they make excellent parents.

Believe it or not, their highly contrasted black coat and white belly actually help to keep them safe. When you look down on a penguin in the water, its black coat helps it blend in with dark water. When you look up at a penguin in the water, its white belly blends in with the bright surface of the water.

Their social nature and distinct appearance helped cause Antarctica to select penguins as the national animal.

BHUTAN

Capital: Thimphu
Official Language: Dzongkha
(a Tibetan dialect)
Population: 736,100

NATIONAL ANIMAL
TAKIN

Height: up to 3.9 feet
Weight: up to 770 pounds
Diet: tough leaves, tree bark, bamboo
Habitat: mountain slopes and thick bamboo forests

HOT AIR

Takins have a very special nose—it warms up the air before it gets to their lungs. This helps them through cold winters in the Himalayan Mountains.

Bhutan selected this unique-looking creature as its national animal because it originated right in Bhutan. Legend says that one of Bhutan's spiritual leaders took a cow and a goat, snapped his fingers, and the takin appeared!

Takins are mammals with hooves, like sheep, goats, and cows. Even though the takin is big and bulky, it can use its hooves to nimbly navigate the rocky mountainous areas. Its skin makes an oily substance that acts like a raincoat to keep its fur dry.

CHINA

Capital: Beijing
Official Language: Mandarin Chinese
Population: 1,390,691,000

BAMBOO BINGE

Pandas eat 28 pounds of bamboo each day—and it takes them exactly half the day to do it!

NATIONAL ANIMAL
GIANT PANDA

Height: 4–5 feet tall
Weight: 300 pounds
Top Speed: 20 miles per hou
Diet: bamboo
Habitat: bamboo forests

China is proud of this rare animal, which is considered to be a "living fossil." One has appeared on China's gold panda bullion coins since 1982, and a panda was chosen as one of thefive mascots of the 2008 Beijing Olympics.

Pandas don't like to spend much time with other pandas and they tend to be shy around humans. In fact, males use their sense of smell to avoid one another. We often see pictures of pandas sitting down, but they're excellent at swimming and climbing trees.

INDIA

Capital: New Delhi
Official Languages:
English, Hindi
Population: 1,364,612,000

SOOTHING SALVE

The tiger's saliva can help cuts heal. When they get injured, licking the wound can stop bleeding and help it heal faster.

NATIONAL ANIMAL
ROYAL BENGAL TIGER

Length: 5–6 feet
Weight: 240–500 pounds
Top Speed: 35–40 miles per hour
Diet: buffalo, deer, wild pigs, and other large mammals
Habitat: tropical rain forests, marshes, and tall grasses

The tiger represents power and elegance. It has been India's national symbol for hundreds of years. Centuries ago, tigers were even worshipped. The goddess Durga was said to ride around on a tiger's back. Tigers appear on Indian money and postage stamps today.

Tigers usually hunt at night. They use their stripes to blend in to the tall grasses before pouncing on their prey. Their long tails help them keep their balance.

INDONESIA

Capital: Jakarta
Official Language: Indonesian
Population: 267,162,000

SCENT-SATIONAL SENSES

Dragons can see objects from 985 feet away, but they mainly hunt using their sense of smell. They can smell meat up to 2.5 miles.

NATIONAL ANIMAL
KOMODO DRAGON

Length: 10 feet
Weight: 330 pounds
Top Speed: 13 miles per hour
Diet: any kind of meat, whether alive or dead (including other Komodo dragons!)
Habitat: tropical savanna forests

Because the Komodo dragon only lives in Indonesia, it acts as a symbol of wildlife for the country. Indonesians call it *oras*, or "land crocodile." It is the heaviest lizard on earth, and can be traced back in history for millions of years.

Komodo dragons will eat almost anything—deer, pigs, smaller dragons, and even humans! They lie still and wait for prey to pass by. Then they jump and take down animals with their sharp teeth and claws. Their mouths inject venom into their prey, which sends the victim into shock.

Capital: Tokyo
Official Language: No official language, but Japanese is the accepted national language
Population: 126,560,000

NATIONAL BIRD

GREEN PHEASANT

Wingspan: 23–34 inches
Length: 20–36 inches
Weight: 2–4 pounds
Top Speed: 35–45 miles per hour
Diet: seeds, berries, fruit, insects, worms, and small reptiles
Habitat: grassy, bushy areas and light forest areas

FEATHERED SEISMOGRAPHS

Pheasants can feel the earth moving before humans do, so they can alert humans about upcoming earthquakes!

The green pheasant appears in Japanese folktales as a messenger of Amaterasu, the sun goddess. Since Amaterasu ruled the heavens, the pheasant represents power, abundance, and promise. It is celebrated in Japan for its courage and its fierce protection of its chicks. Sometimes females even adopt lost chicks.

Pheasants stay in their homes during cold weather. They can dig one foot in the snow to find food, and they can survive without food for several days. In the summer, they breathe a little faster to get rid of excess heat.

PAKISTAN

Capital: Islamabad
Official Languages:
English, Urdu
Population: 214,249,000

The markhor uses its horns for fighting, digging, and removing bark from trees.

NATIONAL ANIMAL
MARKHOR

Height: 2–4 feet
Weight: 70–242 pounds
Top Speed: 10 miles per hour
Diet: grasses, shrub leaves, and twigs
Habitat: mountains

This mountain goat almost became extinct because so many people hunted it—for its meat, to use it as a trophy, and to make medicine from its horns. Special programs limited hunting, and the markhor population grew by 20 percent in 10 years.

Markhor is a Persian word that means "snake killer." The animal may have been given that name because it can easily kill snakes with its wide hooves—or because its curly antlers look like snakes. Those wide hooves also help the markhor balance. It is a big, heavy animal, but is skilled at climbing steep, rocky cliffs. They've also been known to climb trees to look for food!

Capital: Doha
Official Language: Arabic
Population: 2,716,000

NATIONAL ANIMAL
ORYX

Shoulder Height: 2.6–4.1 feet
Weight: 220–460 pounds
Top Speed: 37 miles per hour
Diet: coarse grasses and thorny shrubs
Habitat: desert, semi desert, dry grasslands, and scrublands

BUSY BOTTOM

An oryx's tail swishes all the time—even when the animal is resting!

The oryx was almost extinct 40 years ago—people even thought that the last oryx had died in 1972!—but a conservation program helped it survive. It is the largest wild animal on the Arabian Peninsula, and it's a big part of the culture there. An oryx (named Orry!) was chosen as the official mascot for the 2006 Asian Games in Doha, and you can also see it on Qatar Airways planes.

When you see an oryx from the side, its two horns seem to merge into one. For this reason, some people think this animal inspired the legend of the unicorn.

UNITED ARAB EMIRATES

Capital: Abu Dhabi
Official Language: Arabic
Population: 10,161,000

FIRST-CLASS FLYERS

These falcons are the only animals in the United Arab Emirates allowed to travel inside planes—but only if they're in business class or first class.

NATIONAL BIRD
PEREGRINE FALCON

Wingspan: 39.4–43.3 inches
Top Speed: 200 miles per hour on a dive
Diet: a wide variety of birds
Habitat: open country from tundra to desert to mountains, usually near coastlines

Because peregrine falcons can be trained to deliver prey without killing it first, they have been an essential way people have gathered food for over 1,000 years. The Emerati people believe that falcons stand for courage. You can see this bird on airplanes, postage stamps, company logos, driver's licenses, and more.

They almost became extinct about 70 years ago because of pesticide poisoning, but falconers helped increase their numbers.

Peregrine falcons are super fast. When they power dive to grab prey, they may reach speeds of 200 miles per hour—which makes them the world's fastest animal!

VIETNAM

Capital: Hanoi
Official Language: Vietnamese
Population: 94,685,000

NATIONAL ANIMAL
WATER BUFFALO

Shoulder Height: 5–6.2 feet
Weight: 1,500–2,650 pounds
Top Speed: 30 miles per hour
Diet: grass, herbs, and vegetation
Habitat: tropical and subtropical forests, marshes, wetlands, and swamps

BOTTOM BITERS

The water buffalo doesn't have any top teeth in its mouth!

Water buffalos are called "the tractors of the East" because they have helped plow fields and transport people for over 5,000 years. The Vietnamese appreciate their hard work, their gentle nature, and their loyalty.

These massive animals are thought to bring good fortune, too. If a water buffalo's hair is growing evenly and symmetrically, it means good luck and good health.

Water buffalo milk can make real mozzarella cheese! It's so popular that Italian pizza and pasta restaurants have appeared in many Vietnamese cities.

AUSTRALIA

Capital: Canberra
Official Language: No official language, but English is the accepted national language
Population: 24,995,000

NATIONAL ANIMAL
RED KANGAROO

UNBELIEVABLE BOUNCE

Height: 3.25–5.25 feet
Weight: 200 pounds
Top Speed: over 35 miles per hour
Diet: grasses and shrubs
Habitat: deserts and open grasslands

Red kangaroos can jump six feet off the ground and move 25 feet in a single jump!

The indigenous peoples of Australia hunted kangaroos for thousands of years—even the word kangaroo comes from the language of the first people there. British explorers who came to Australia in the 1700s described the kangaroo as having the head of a deer and the hop of a frog.

You'll find kangaroos on the Australian coat of arms, airplanes, logos, coins, stamps, and more. Because kangaroos have a difficult time walking backward, they represent moving forward.

Kangaroos may look cuddly and cute, but they bite and have sharp claws. Males sometimes rest their weight on their tails so they can use their strong legs to "box" each other.

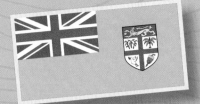

Capital: Suva
Official Languages:
English, Hindi, iTaukei
(Fijian)
Population: 888,700

NATIONAL BIRD
COLLARED LORY

Wingspan: 18 inches
Height: 8 inches
Weight: 2.5 − −3.2 ounces
Diet: fruit, seeds, nectar, and blossoms
Habitat: forests, mangroves, and eucalyptus groves

ASHIONABLE FEATHERS

This parrot got its name because of the long feathers at the back of its neck stand up like a collar.

This bird is native to Fiji (where it's called **kula** or **parrot of paradise**), and it's the only rain forest bird that has adapted to living in cities. It appears on Fiji's dollar coin.

Even though they have brightly colored feathers, the lory's colors provide camouflage in the colorful forest. They have been traditionally used as decoration by the people of Samoa and Tonga. The collared lory's tongue has a brush at the end to sweep up nectar. It is a fast flier, and it tends to be a bit shy. The collared lory makes a soft whistling noise.

NEW ZEALAND

Capital: Wellington
Official Languages: English, Maori, New Zealand Sign Language
Population: 4,889,000

NATIONAL ANIMAL
KIWI

Wingspan: 16-24 inches
Height: 14–25 inches
Weight: 1.9–11 pounds
Diet: worms, crayfish, berries, seeds, and some leaves
Habitat: steep, wet forests of New Zealand

FLIGHTLESS FEATHERS

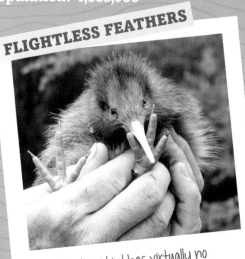

The kiwi bird has virtually no wings and no tail!

Many countries have a national animal and a national bird, but in New Zealand, one animal captured both titles! The kiwi bird had stood as a symbol of New Zealand for more than 100 years. During World War I, New Zealand soldiers wore military badges featuring an image of a kiwi. Soldiers from other countries called them "Kiwis" and by World War II, the name was associated with all New Zealanders. The term is a symbol of pride and endearment within the country.

New Zealand's Maori people have said that the bird is a *taonga* (treasure) and used its feathers to weave a special cloak worn by chiefs. The country is so protective of their national animal that they celebrate Save Kiwi Month every October.

Capital: Port Moresby
Official Languages: English, Hiri Motu, Pisin, Tok
Population: 8,288,000

CURIOUS COUSINS

The dugong's closest relative on land is the elephant.

NATIONAL ANIMAL
DUGONG

Length: 8–10 feet
Weight: 510–1,100 pounds
Top Speed: 14 miles per hour
Diet: underwater grasses
Habitat: warm coastal waters from East Africa to Australia

Dugongs are sometimes called "sea cows" and they can live for up to 70 years. Scientists have found sea cow fossils near the island of New Guinea that are 12 million years old!

Once upon a time, sailors thought dugongs were mermaids—they even wrote poems to them.

Some island tribes think the dugong's size and strength make it a spirit being or sacred animal. Some tribes have used the animal's bones and teeth in religious ceremonies, but other groups forbid hunting them. Dugongs almost became extinct, but declaring them as the national animal gave them extra protection.

CROATIA

Capital: Zagreb
Official Language: Croatian
Population: 4,081,000

CAR WRECKERS

Martens tear apart wires, plugs, and windshield wipers. They are such a threat to cars that in some places, drivers can purchase insurance to protect themselves from martens.

NATIONAL ANIMAL
MARTEN

Height: about 6 inches
Weight: 2.2–4.4 pounds
Diet: voles, mice, birds, eggs, insects, frogs, honey, fungi, and berries
Habitat: wooded areas and rocky hillsides

Centuries ago, people used to trade the marten's fur for cash. Because of the animal's value, Croatians have called their money the *kuna* (meaning "marten") since the mid-thirteenth century. Their coins even feature a marten on them.

Martens mostly hunt for food at night. During the day, the marten takes shelter in a hollow tree or abandoned nest to avoid predators. Humans have been decreasing the number of martens by cutting down their forest homes.

CYPRUS

Capital: Lefkosia
Official Languages: Greek, Turkish
Population: 1,223,400

CYPRUS MOUFLON

Shoulder Height: 3 feet
Weight: 35–50 pounds
Diet: soft tender roots, wild berries, and weeds
Habitat: the mountainous Paphos Forest on Cyprus

HIGH-UP HIDEOUTS

When these goats are being chased, they climb steep cliffs for protection.

Some people believe these wild sheep have been living in Cyprus for thousands of years. The animal's image has appeared on ancient pottery, stamps, coins, and more. In 1878, there were only 15 mouflon left. Because of special anti-hunting rules, there are now 3,000.

The mouflon are friendly, but very shy and very fast, so it's often difficult to find one. Some farmers tame them and put bells around their necks.

ENGLAND

Capital: London
Official Language: No official language, but English is the accepted national language
Population: 53,012,456

UNRELATED

Despite similar names and appearance, the European robin and the American robin are actually from two different families of birds!

NATIONAL BIRD
EUROPEAN ROBIN

Wingspan: 8–9 inches
Length: 5–6 inches
Weight: .5–.8 ounces
Top Speed: 18 miles per hour
Diet: insects, earthworms, fruits and berries
Habitat: parks and gardens, spruce woods in northern Europe

England is part of the United Kingdom, along with Wales, Scotland and Northern Ireland, but maintains many of its own symbols.

The European robin was chosen as the national bird of Britain during a nationwide ballot in 2015. More than 200,000 people voted for the robin, which claimed the top spot over the barn owl and the blackbird. Not only is the robin a common sight in Britain, but it is widely featured in British folklore and children's stories.

During the Victorian era, postmen in Britain wore red jackets, which earned them the nickname "Robins." When delivering Christmas cards, people said they were carried by robins, meaning the postmen. The birds have been associated with Christmas ever since.

Capital: Tallinn
Official Language: Estonian
Population: 1,319,000

NATIONAL ANIMAL
GRAY WOLF

Height: 36–63 inches
Weight: 40–175 pounds
Top Speed: 36–38 miles per hour
Diet: deer, mountain goats, moose, elk, and bison
Habitat: tundra, mountain areas, woodlands, forests, grasslands, and deserts

VORACIOUS APPETITE

A wolf can eat 20 pounds of meat in a single meal, which is like a human eating one hundred hamburgers!

Several Estonian nature organizations voted the wolf as the national animal in 2018. It beat the beaver, the badger, the fox, the hedgehog, and the roe deer. The wolf is considered tough, clever, charismatic, and a survivor. The wolf is the most represented animal in Estonian folklore and the country's bogs and forests are sometimes called "wolf lands".

Wolves are the largest members of the dog family, and they are known for their howl. Wolves travel in packs, and each pack has a territory. There are about 200 wolves in Estonia.

FINLAND

Capital: Helsinki
Official Language: No official language, but Finnish and Swedish are the accepted national languages
Population: 5,518,000

NATIONAL ANIMAL
WHOOPER SWAN

Wingspan: 8.2 feet
Weight: 24 pounds
Diet: aquatic plants and roots
Habitat: freshwater lakes, pools, shallow rivers, marshes, bogs, and swamps

WHOOP IT UP!

This animal's "whooping" call is one of the loudest among birds.

The national *animal* of Finland is the brown bear, but Finland's national bird is the whooper swan.
You can find the whooper swan on the Finnish Euro coin. It represents cleanliness, reliability, and strength.

The whooper swan is one of the heaviest flying birds. Some swans spend the whole year in Finland, while others fly south for the winter.

Hunters almost wiped out the whooper swan population, but conservation efforts began in the 1950s to save the bird.

FRANCE

Capital: Paris
Official Language: French
Population: 65,097,000

NATIONAL ANIMAL
GALLIC ROOSTER

Wingspan: 1–1.5 feet
Weight: 6.5 pounds
Top Speed: 9 miles per hour
Diet: cereals, worms, insects
Habitat: temperate climates

FUTILE FLIGHT

The rooster can only fly for about 200 feet.

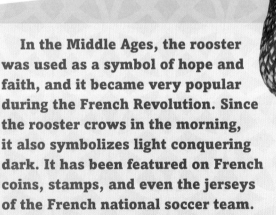

In the Middle Ages, the rooster was used as a symbol of hope and faith, and it became very popular during the French Revolution. Since the rooster crows in the morning, it also symbolizes light conquering dark. It has been featured on French coins, stamps, and even the jerseys of the French national soccer team.

But what *is* a rooster? It's an adult male chicken. You can find roosters on every continent except Antarctica. They have been crowing for about 5,000 years!

GREECE

Capital: Athens
Official Language: Greek
Population: 10,756,000

NATIONAL ANIMAL
DOLPHIN

When dolphins "sleep," they rest one side of the brain at a time. This allows them to continue to watch for predators and get air from the surface.

Length: 6.5 feet–13 feet
Weight: 220–660 pounds
Top Speed: 25 miles per hour
Diet: fish
Habitat: ocean

Dolphins are so much a part of Greek culture that they appear in ancient Greek mythology. They were messengers of Poseidon, god of the sea, and were considered sacred by Aphrodite and Apollo. An ancient Greek coin depicts Poseidon's son Taurus riding on the back of a dolphin.

Dolphins have been known to help other animals and people in need, even bringing them to the surface to breathe if they've been underwater too long. They're very social animals—they live in groups and work together to find food and raise children. The Greek people admire the dolphin's intelligence and friendliness.

HUNGARY

Capital: Budapest
Official Language: Hungarian
Population: 9,725,000

Hungary has 195 statues of the Turul.

NATIONAL ANIMAL
TURUL

The Turul isn't real! The Turul bird is a mythical bird of prey that often looks like a falcon. One ancient story says that this bird is the father of a line of Hungarian rulers. Another legend says that the Turul dropped its sword in Budapest, telling the original Hungarians that the land was to be their home.

The Turul is a national symbol of guidance and togetherness. It can be found in the coats of arms of the Hungarian army, the Counter Terrorism Center, and the Office of National Security. You can also find the Turul's image on shirts, flags, clocks, and more.

ICELAND

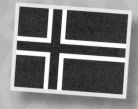

Capital: Reykjavik
Official Language:
Icelandic
Population: 353,600

NATIONAL ANIMAL
GYRFALCON

Wingspan: 4–4.5 feet
Weight: 2–4.5 pounds
Top Speed: 90–150 miles per hour
Diet: ptarmigan, sage grouse, jaegers, gulls, terns, fulmars, auks, pheasants, hawks, owls, ravens, and songbirds
Habitat: tundra

ARISTOCRATIC AVIATORS

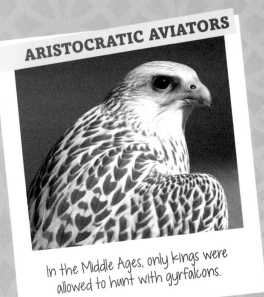

In the Middle Ages, only kings were allowed to hunt with gyrfalcons.

This hunting bird has been worshipped as far back as Viking times, and medieval kings owned gyrfalcons as a sign of power. They represent beauty, power, and freedom.

The gyrfalcon is the largest falcon in the world. Gyrfalcons can be a variety of colors—from white to pure black. Few predators hunt the gyrfalcon. Humans are its biggest threat.

Because arctic temperatures have increased, the peregrine falcon may be traveling farther north than ever before, which means these two falcons may end up fighting for a limited amount of nests in the same area.

Capital: Dublin
Official Languages:
English, Irish
Population: 4,834,000

NATIONAL ANIMAL
RED DEER

Shoulder Height: 3.2–5 feet
Weight: 300–550 pounds
Diet: grass, herbs, tree shoots, acorns, and fruits
Habitat: woodlands and open grassland

WAY TO GROW!

Deer antlers can grow two inches a day!

Red deer are the only species of deer native to Ireland. They have made their home there since 10,000 BCE. No two sets of antlers are identical, and antler shape can be used to identify deer.

Though red deer have good eyesight and a strong sense of hearing, they rely on their sense of smell the most. Mothers and babies communicate through scent glands located under their eyes.

Because of **deforestation**, many herds almost became extinct, but the government has been working to help the deer population grow.

ROMANIA

Capital: Bucharest
Official Language: Romanian
Population: 19,438,000

Lynx have short light-brown or red fur in the summer and long silver-gray fur in the winter.

NATIONAL ANIMAL
LYNX

Length: up to 3.3 feet
Weight: 66–88 pounds
Top Speed: 50 miles per hour
Diet: deer, rabbits, and birds
Habitat: hills or mountain forests

These big cats are quiet, nocturnal and so secretive that they almost seem invisible. Because of hunting and deforestation, the number of lynx is dropping. Romania selected the lynx as its national animal to give it added protection.

Lynx usually hunt and rest alone. They have excellent hearing, which helps them find prey and avoid predators. Their paws act like snowshoes to help them travel through deep snow. They are powerful, and can bring down prey four times their size.

Capital: Moscow
Official Language: Russian
Population: 144,825,000

NATIONAL ANIMAL

BROWN BEAR

Length: 4.6–9.2 feet
Weight: 180–1300 pounds
Top Speed: 30 miles per hour
Diet: rodents, moose, nuts, fruits, berries, and leaves
Habitat: arctic tundra

EXTREME DIET

Brown bears lose up to half their weight during hibernation.

The bear symbolizes strength, endurance, and resilience. But it can also be cute! During the 1980 Olympics in Moscow, the mascot was a cuddly illustrated brown bear named Misha. Misha was the first Olympic mascot to reach large-scale success, appearing on stamps, T-shirts, and even a cartoon!

The brown bear has a hump on its shoulders to store the energy it needs to move rocks and claw through cold, hard soil to find food. Females hibernate all winter long—they won't even wake up when they give birth!

SCOTLAND

Capital: Edinburgh
Official Languages: English, Scots Gaelic
Population: 5,295,400

WISHFUL THINKING

People thought the unicorn was real until 1825, when a scientist proved that unicorns couldn't possibly exist.

NATIONAL ANIMAL
UNICORN

Because history, myths, and legends are popular in Scotland, it's no surprise that their country's national animal is the unicorn! One Scottish myth says that after a snake poisoned a watering hole, a unicorn appeared, dipped its horn in the water, and cleaned the water for all the animals. The myth shows that the unicorn uses its power to protect others.

The unicorn first appeared on the Scottish royal coat of arms in the twelfth century, and it seems more popular than ever today! It represents purity, innocence, power, and kindness. You can see unicorns on fountains, castles, and cathedrals.

SPAIN

Capital: Madrid
Official Language: Castilian Spanish
Population: 46,630,000

NATIONAL ANIMAL

BULL

Height: 5.4 feet
Weight: 660–1100 pounds
Top Speed: 35 miles per hour
Diet: grass and shrubs
Habitat: grasslands

SEEING RED

Bulls, like other cattle, are color-blind to red. It is not the color, but the motion, of the bullfighter's cape that attracts the bull.

Bullfighting is so popular in Spain that it led to the bull being selected as the national animal. Pamplona celebrates the Running of the Bulls every July. The bulls run from outside the city to the bullring, which takes anywhere from two to ten minutes.

There are several types of bulls, but the bull used for fighting is called toro bravo. Some experts say that these bulls are descendants of the bulls used in Roman arena games. Some Spanish people don't support bullfighting because they don't want the bulls to get hurt. Officials in Barcelona, for instance, have declared that it is an "anti-bullfighting city."

BAHAMAS

Capital: **Nassau**
Official Language: **English**
Population: **377,000**

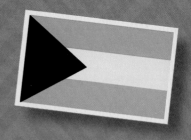

YOU ARE WHAT YOU EAT

Flamingos get their pink color from the food they eat. If they don't eat live shrimp or "flamingo chow," they will turn white.

FLAMINGO

Wingspan: **37–39 inches**
Height: **4–5 feet**
Weight: **4–8 pounds**
Diet: **algae, insect larvae, and tiny animals like shrimp and mollusks**
Habitat: **mudflats or lagoons**

More than 50,000 flamingos live in the Bahamas, and they are protected by the Society for the Protection of the Flamingo. The flamingo appears on the national coat of arms.

To eat, flamingos stir mud with their feet, take a gulp of mud and water, strain small animals out of the mud with their beak, and then spit out the muddy water. They do all of this with their heads upside down!

BELIZE

Capital: Belmopan
Official Language: English
Population: 398,000

FOOD-FOCUSED

The tapir spends 90 percent of its waking hours hunting for food.

NATIONAL ANIMAL
BAIRD'S TAPIR

Height: 6–8 feet
Weight: 330–705 pounds
Top Speed: 30 miles per hour
Diet: leaves, twigs, fruit, and seeds
Habitat: tropical forests, woodlands, grasslands, and marshes

Known as a "mountain cow" in Belize, the tapir is the largest land mammal of Central America. It has a nose like an elephant or anteater, but it is actually related to the horse and rhinoceros. The tapir has looked just about the same for 35 million years!

The tapir moves easily on land and water, and it can even climb steep slopes. Tapirs can't see very well, but they make up for it with their hearing and sense of smell. If they're being followed, they can run as fast as a human.

April the tapir was one of the first ambassadors of the Belize Zoo, and every year, the zoo celebrated her birthday in the month of April. Starting in 2008, Belize started celebrating World Tapir Day on April 27 to raise awareness for this animal.

CANADA

Capital: Ottawa
Official Language: English, French
Population: 37,512,000

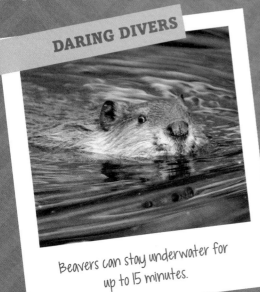

Beavers can stay underwater for up to 15 minutes.

NATIONAL ANIMAL
BEAVER

Length: 2.4–3 feet
Weight: 24–71 pounds
Land Speed: 34 miles per hour
Water Speed: 5 miles per hour
Diet: leaves, bark, twigs, roots, aquatic plants
Habitat: forests, rivers, lakes, streams

The beaver was selected as Canada's national animal in 1975 due to its long history in the region. During the sixteenth century, the beaver fur trade was one of the main economic ventures in North America. The trade was a major industry for 300 years. The beaver is symbolized throughout Canada in places like Montreal's coat of arms, Canada's 5-cent coin, and the country's first postage stamp.

You can find beavers in every Canadian province. They frequently burrow along the edges of rivers and lakes. But if they can't find a place they'd like to live, they make one! Busy beavers gnaw trees, logs, and branches with their strong teeth and jaws to make homes.

COSTA RICA

Capital: San José
Official Language: Spanish
Population: 5,004,000

NATIONAL ANIMAL

WEST INDIAN
MANATEE

Length: 8–13 feet
Weight: 440–1,300 pounds
Top Speed: up to 20 miles
per hour in short bursts
Diet: seagrasses and
other aquatic plants,
sometimes fish
Habitat: shallow,
slow-moving waters
of rivers, estuaries,
saltwater bays, canals

FANTASTIC FLIPPERS

The manatee's flexible flippers help it steer in deep water and help it "walk" in shallow water.

The West Indian manatee lives in the Gulf of Mexico and the Caribbean Sea, but it spends its winters in Florida. It usually returns to the same spot every year. In Costa Rica, you can go diving or snorkeling right next to these gentle giants!

This "sea cow" only has one child in its lifetime, and its numbers are decreasing. In 2013 alone, 20 percent of the population was wiped out. If the manatee disappears completely, many ecosystems will suffer.

EL SALVADOR

Capital: San Salvador
Official Language: Spanish
Population: 6,646,000

NATIONAL ANIMAL
TURQUOISE-BROWED MOTMOT

DEN-DIGGERS

Instead of building nests, these birds dig burrows in the ground.

Weight: 2.3 ounces
Diet: small insects, reptiles, and fruit
Habitat: tropical deciduous forests, savannas, and bushes; also open, dry regions

People in El Salvador call this bird the *Torogoz*. It is popular because of its beauty. It also represents family unity because males and females help raise chicks together.

In some places in the country, you can find these birds rather easily, especially because they live in fairly open areas. The motmot wags its tail back and forth like the pendulum of an old-fashioned clock. It also moves its tail to let predators know that it has spotted them.

Capital: Kingston
Official Language: English
Population: 2,734,000

NATIONAL ANIMAL
DOCTORBIRD

DOCTOR, DOCTOR!

The doctorbird may have been named for its black crest and tails, which look like an old-fashioned doctor's top hat and long coat.

Wingspan: 6.5 inches
Length: 4–11.5 inches
Weight: .16–.18 ounces
Top Speed: 30 miles per hour
Diet: plant nectar, spiders, and insects
Habitat: forests, plantations, parks, and gardens

This colorful hummingbird only lives in Jamaica and has been celebrated with folktales and songs. Early settlers thought the bird had magic powers. Even today, people think that killing a doctorbird will bring bad luck.

Jamaica has 320 species of hummingbirds, and the doctorbird stands out the most. It looks iridescent, with colors that seem to change from different angles.

MEXICO

Capital: Mexico City
Official Language: Spanish
Population: 124,786,000

NATIONAL ANIMAL
XOLOITZCUINTLI

SAY WHAT?

Height: 18–23 inches
Weight: 30–55 pounds
Habitat: indoor house pet

Xoloitzcuintli is pronounced:
"show-low-eats-QUEENT-lee."
Or you can just call it the Xolo!

This dog's history goes back 3,000 years. Ancient Aztecs named them for Xolotl, their dog-headed god. European explorers mentioned seeing these "strange hairless dogs" during their journey to the New World. They're sometimes called the first dog of the Americas.

The xoloitzcuintli is a great watchdog, and it loves people. It's sometimes called a "Velcro dog" because it's so attached to its owner. This dog can pick up on its owner's feelings, and it has been called a "doctor" in Mexico because the heat its body gives off is comforting to people with arthritis.

UNITED STATES

Capital: Washington, DC
Official Language: No official language, but English is the accepted national language
Population: 328,523,000

NATIONAL ANIMAL

AMERICAN BISON

Height: 7–11.5 feet
Weight: 930–2,200 pounds
Top Speed: 40 miles per hour
Diet: grasses, herbs, shrubs, and twigs
Habitat: grasslands and prairie

A.K.A.

Baby bison are nicknamed "red dogs" because they're born with red-brown hair.

Even though the bison was declared the national mammal in 2016, it has lived in what is now the Yellowstone National Park since prehistoric times, and has been very important to Native American culture. In 1992, the InterTribal Buffalo Council was established to transfer bison from national park lands to tribal lands. The American Bison Society was formed in 1905, in part by President Theodore Roosevelt, to help save the bison from extinction.

Bison are the largest mammal in North America. They have a great sense of hearing and smell, but they can't see very well. A whole herd might stampede if startled. If you see a bison's tail standing straight up . . . be careful! That means it's ready to charge!

ARGENTINA

Capital: Buenos Aires
Official Language: Spanish
Population: 44,495,000

NATIONAL ANIMAL
RED OVENBIRD

Wingspan: 7.5–10.2 inches
Height: 4.3–5.5 inches
Weight: 18–49 grams
Diet: small bugs, larvae, spiders, and worms
Habitat: forests

SERENDIPITOUS SOUNDS

In addition to being good at construction, red ovenbirds are beautiful singers. Hearing their song is said to bring good luck.

Scientists and naturalists who met in Buenos Aires in 1916 chose this bird as their ambassador, which led to it being selected as Argentina's national bird in 1928. They picked the rufous hornero because of its fascinating nest-making ability. Its nests look like old-fashioned wood-fired ovens. They're built in many stages, and they can survive storms. A South American proverb goes, "No thunder ever fell where horneros have nested."

The people of Argentina appreciate the hornero's beauty, intelligence, and craftsmanship.

BRAZIL

Capital: Brasilia
Official Language: Portuguese
Population: 208,495,000

POWERFUL PREDATOR

The jaguar's name comes from the Native American name yaguar, which means "he who kills with one leap."

NATIONAL ANIMAL
JAGUAR

Length: 5–6 feet
Weight: 100–250 pounds
Top Speed: 40 miles per hour
Diet: tapirs, birds, sloths, turtles, rodents, reptiles, monkeys, frogs, and deer
Habitat: rain forests, dense swamplands, and wetlands

The jaguar is at the top of its food chain and represents speed and strength. It can swim or climb trees to find food. Its powerful jaws are strong enough to crack a sea turtle's shell. Jaguars help control the ecosystem in Brazil.

The jaguar's spots are called "rosettes." Jaguars resemble leopards, but you can tell these animals apart because jaguars' rosettes have spots inside them and leopards' rosettes don't.

BOLIVIA

Capital: La Paz (administrative), Sucre (constitutional)
Official Languages: Spanish, 36 native languages
Population: 11,307,000

LLAMA

Height: 5.5-6 feet
Weight: 250 pounds
Top Speed: 28 miles per hour
Diet: grass and plants
Habitat: mountains and rocky areas

PLEASANT POOP

Llama poop doesn't smell! Farmers call it "llama beans."

Llamas are camelids—that means that they're related to camels. They don't need a lot of water and they survive by eating lots of different types of plants. Llamas have been used as pack animals for over 4,000 years. They can travel up to 20 miles a day while carrying loads of 50 to 75 pounds. But if you ask them to carry too much, they might lie down and refuse to move!

The llama has served many purposes for the Bolivian people: transportation, meat, wool, leather, and fuel. Llamas and their wool are used by *curanderos*, which means medicine men or healers, to help people.

CHILE

Capital: Santiago
Official Language: Spanish
Population: 17,967,000

NATIONAL ANIMAL

HUEMUL DEER

Shoulder Height: 3.2 feet
Weight: up to 198 pounds
Top Speed: 37–50 miles per hour
Diet: buds and tender leaves of herbs, shrubs, bushes, and trees
Habitat: rugged mountainous areas

BASHFUL BROWSER

The huemul deer is so shy that most Chileans will never see one.

The huemul deer has short legs to maintain its balance on the rocky, uneven ground. Its coat is oily, and each hair is hollow. This helps keep it warm as it swims through water, and it also helps it dry off quickly once it gets out of the water.

This deer can eat lots of different types of plants, but it prefers more tender leaves. Because of this preference, the deer is called a "browser."

Native to Chile, the huemul deer appears on Chile's national coat of arms. Because there are less than 2,000 deer left, Chileans are working hard to save the species. Hunting, predator attacks, and habitat destruction have been responsible for the decrease in population.

GUATEMALA

Capital: Guatemala City
Official Language: Spanish
Population: 17,316,000

NATIONAL ANIMAL
QUETZAL BIRD

LIVE FREE!

The quetzal bird represents liberty. People say it will die of sadness if caged.

Wingspan: 16 inches
Height: 15–16 inches
Weight: 7–8 ounces
Diet: fruit, insects, lizards, and other small creatures
Habitat: mountainous, tropical forests

The quetzal was sacred to ancient Maya and Aztec peoples, and royalty and priests wore its feathers. It is one of the spirit guides for the Maya. Its name means "precious" or "sacred," and it is a symbol of goodness and light.

The quetzal is considered to be one of the most beautiful birds in the world. Its two tail feathers can grow to be three feet long. It became the national bird of Guatemala in 1871, and it is celebrated every year on September 5. Guatemalan money is also called "quetzal."

PERU

Capital: Lima
Official Languages: Aymara, Spanish, Quechua
Population: 31,358,000

NATIONAL ANIMAL
VICUÑA

Height: 2.5–2.8 feet
Weight: 77–130 pounds
Top Speed: 30 miles per hour
Diet: grasses
Habitat: grasslands and savannas with few trees or bushes at least 11,000 feet above sea level

SLEEPY SNACKERS

Vicuña babies sometimes graze while lying down.

Ancient Incans had laws protecting vicuñas. When the Spanish conquered the area, they removed hunting restrictions and the vicuña population dropped. Now its numbers are growing because law once again protects it. You can see the vicuña on the crest of the Peruvian flag.

Vicuña wool is one of the most expensive types of wool in the world because it is extremely soft and warm. Incans considered it to be the "cloth of gold," and only royalty were allowed to wear it. Today, a vicuña wool sweatshirt might cost about $24,000.

VENEZUELA

Capital: Caracas
Official Languages: Castilian Spanish.
Indigenous languages hold official
status within their respective villages.
Population: 31,828,000

When troupials sing, they perch high up
in the trees where they can be seen
by other animals.

NATIONAL ANIMAL
TROUPIA

Wingspan: 4 inches
Height: 9–10 inches
Weight: 2–2.3 ounces
Diet: insects, fruit, nectar,
berries, and seeds
Habitat: woodland
habitats with lush, dense
vegetation

The troupial is a member of
the "New World Oriole" family.
It can produce a beautiful melody,
and it can also mimic the sounds of
other birds.

Troupials are nest pirates—they
steal nests from other birds rather
than building their own. Then they
redecorate according to their needs,
and they fiercely protect their stolen nest
from getting stolen by another animal.

More than 1,300 birds have been spotted
in Venezuela—they help bring tourists to
the country on bird-watching trips.

SAVE THE ANIMALS!

We've traveled from the ocean to the mountaintops. From the tundra to the desert. We've explored 7 continents and met 55 animals that tell us a lot about what each country values.

But there's one national animal that you haven't met . . .

Did you know that one national animal is extinct? The dodo bird was a chubby, clumsy, flightless bird from the pigeon family that was native to Mauritius, a small island in the Indian Ocean. When Dutch settlers arrived in the 1600s, they brought new diseases and new animals like pigs, goats, and monkeys that either ate dodo eggs or competed with dodos for food. As a result, the dodo was extinct within 100 years.

Of all the national animals of the world, 35 are extinct, endangered, or critically endangered. Another 48 animals are labeled as "vulnerable," which means that they are on their way to becoming endangered. It's up to us to make sure other animals don't go "the way of the dodo" and disappear.

Being chosen as a national animal often helps endangered species by giving them a lot of attention—the whole country wants to help them survive. The oryx, the huemul deer, and the vicuña are three examples of national animals that were helped by conservation efforts.

Zoos also help national animals survive. They make sure animals get the right amount of food and care, and they try to reintroduce healthy animals into the wild. Although you won't see a dodo at the zoo, you may find other creatures that you've read about in this book. So the next time you go to the zoo, keep your eyes open for these special animals!

GLOSSARY

Burrows: holes in the ground that animals turn into homes

Conservation: protecting things found in nature

Currents: movements or flow

Deforestation: cutting down forests

Extinction: when animals disappear from Earth completely

Falconers: people who train birds of prey

Hemisphere: one half of Earth

Iridescent: color appears to change as the angle or light changes

Mammals: animals that breathe air, have a backbone, and grow hair

Native: an animal that originally grew or lived in a place

Poachers: people who take or kill wild animals illegally

Predators: animals that hunt, catch, and eat other animals

Prey: animals that are hunted, caught, and eaten by other animals

Pride: a group of lions

Primates: a group of intelligent mammals that includes lemurs, monkeys, apes, and humans

Province: a smaller part of a country

Radiate: spread or send out

Territory: a nesting site occupied by an animal or a group of animals

Venom: a toxic substance produced by animals to injure other animals